DATE		

The
Great Chicago Fire

by Marc Tyler Nobleman

Content Adviser: Martha Gardner, Ph.D.,
Assistant Professor, Department of History,
DePaul University

Reading Adviser: Rosemary G. Palmer, Ph.D.,
Department of Literacy, College of Education,
Boise State University

COMPASS POINT BOOKS
MINNEAPOLIS, MINNESOTA

Compass Point Books
3109 West 50th Street, #115
Minneapolis, MN 55410

Visit Compass Point Books on the Internet at *www.compasspointbooks.com*
or e-mail your request to *custserv@compasspointbooks.com*

On the cover: Chicagoans flee the burning city in an 1870s Currier & Ives lithograph.

Photographs ©: Library of Congress, cover, back cover, 20, 22, 35; Prints Old & Rare, back cover (far left); Chicago Historical Society, 5, 7, 17, 26; Corbis, 6, 14; Hulton Archive/Getty Images, 9; The New York Public Library/Art Resource, N.Y., 10; North Wind Picture Archives, 12, 24, 27, 38, 39; Bettmann/Corbis, 13, 30, 31, 33, 40; The Granger Collection, New York, 18; Stock Montage, 23, 25; PhotoDisc, 36; James P. Rowan, 41.

Editor: Jennifer VanVoorst
Designer/Page Production: Bradfordesign, Inc./Bobbie Nuytten
Photo Researcher: Svetlana Zhurkin
Cartographer: XNR Productions, Inc.
Educational Consultant: Diane Smolinski
Library Consultant: Kathleen Baxter

Managing Editor: Catherine Neitge
Creative Director: Keith Griffin
Editorial Director: Carol Jones

Library of Congress Cataloging-in-Publication Data
Nobleman, Marc Tyler.
  The Great Chicago Fire / by Marc Tyler Nobleman.
      p. cm.— (We the people)
  Includes bibliographical references and index.
  ISBN 0-7565-1263-8 (hardcover)
1. Great Fire, Chicago, Ill., 1871—Juvenile literature. 2. Fires—Illinois—Chicago—History—19th century—Juvenile literature. 3. Chicago (Ill.)—History—To 1875—Juvenile literature. I. Title. II. Series: We the people (Series) (Compass Point Books)
  F548.42.N63 2006
  977.3'11—dc22   2005002462

TABLE OF CONTENTS

Red Snowflakes 4

Queen of the West 8

A Giant Tinderbox 11

The Cow 16

The Night Chicago Died 21

Fireproof Spirit 28

The Real Cause 34

A Brand-New City 38

Glossary 42

Did You Know? 43

Important Dates 44

Important People 45

Want to Know More? 46

Index 48

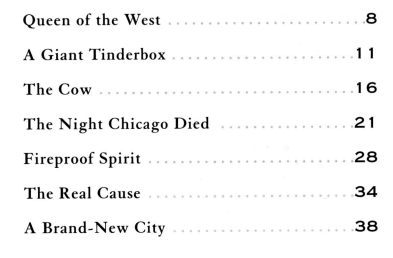

RED SNOWFLAKES

On a Sunday night in October 1871, 13-year-old Bessie Bradwell jolted up in bed. Her mother Myra, a publisher and lawyer, and her father James, a judge, also awakened. Like Bessie, they sensed that something was not right. When they looked outside, they saw that their city of Chicago, Illinois, was on fire.

Bessie's family frantically packed a trunk with their belongings. Bessie wanted to save her best clothes from the fire, so she put them on. The Bradwells left their home, not knowing if it would survive the fire.

The fire seemed to be everywhere. Bessie thought it looked like a snowstorm, only with red flakes instead of white. Panicked people jammed the streets, carrying whatever items were valuable to them. One man was carrying a crate of live chickens over his head. Others were empty-handed, focused on saving nothing more than their own lives. In the confusion, Bessie and her family were separated.

4

A group gathers on the North Side in this painting by a survivor of the Great Fire.

Friends of Bessie's parents spotted her. They were headed for one of the bridges that crossed over the river that snaked through the city. They urged Bessie to come with them, and she did. Though the bridge was burning, it was still passable. Bessie's coat caught fire, but strangers nearby patted it out with their hands. As they crossed, she heard a man say, "This is the end of Chicago."

"No, no," Bessie said, "she will rise again." She turned back and saw huge waves of flame sweeping over the city.

Meanwhile, Bessie's father and mother had also separated. Her father ran to his office to rescue his collection of rare law books while her mother waited for him at the lakefront at the edge of the city. Many people gathered there, wetting their faces in the lake water to combat the intense heat. When James realized that he could not save his books, he hurried to the lake and located Myra.

"Where is Bessie?" he asked.

"I thought she was with you," Myra said. James feared the worst, but Myra was optimistic. She felt that somehow Bessie would be all right.

Myra Bradwell

James Bradwell

The city was in pieces, but Bessie was safe with her parents' friends. The next morning, she set off by herself to look for her parents, but she did not find them.

Fires burned throughout the city until late the next day. The night following the fire, James attended a citizens' meeting. He announced that he lost his little girl. But another man at the meeting had met Bessie on her search. This man knew exactly where Bessie was and told James that she was safe. Thanks to that man, the Bradwells reunited. However, the Great Fire did not spare every Chicago family from tragedy.

7

QUEEN OF THE WEST

Before Chicago burned, it boomed. The American Civil War ended in 1865, and since that time the city had been growing quickly. Railroads had become the dominant mode of transportation and shipping. Ten of them met in Chicago, making the city a critical hub connecting the East and West coasts and one of the most important cities in the country. One song referred to Chicago as the "Queen of the West."

The railroads prompted the creation of factories and meatpacking plants, which in turn created jobs. To fill those jobs, immigrants from Germany, Ireland, Russia, and many other countries poured into Chicago. Each ethnic group settled in one of the three sections of the city. Neighborhoods in the northern, southern, and western sides of the city each took on the uniqueness or personality of the individual cultures. Though conditions in the factories were harsh, people needed work to make

Country farmers sold their crops in Haymarket Square, in Chicago's Near West Side.

a better life for themselves and their families.

Chicago seemed to have everything that made a city thrive. It had a vibrant multicultural population, a large industrial district, a bustling financial district, and a location that was on the way to almost anywhere. It also

9

boasted another feature that was not typical of Midwestern cities: a shoreline. It was situated along Lake Michigan, a body of water so large that a person might mistake it for an ocean. The Chicago River wound through the center of the city.

Chicago was nicknamed the "Windy City," but it also could have been called the "Water City." Yet on the night of October 8, 1871, all that water could not prevent Chicago from becoming a city of fire.

The Chicago River flows into Lake Michigan at the Port of Chicago.

A GIANT TINDERBOX

In early October 1871, conditions in Chicago were ripe for fire. Less than 2 inches (5 centimeters) of rain had fallen on Chicago since July 3. Thousands of buildings, row after row, were made from wood or had wood trim. Out of 88 miles (141 kilometers) of paved streets, 57 miles (91 km) were paved with wood. More than 500 miles (800 km) of sidewalks were also wood-paved. Stacks of lumber were piled in yards of mills and homes.

Some people realized that this combination of factors could turn Chicago into a giant tinderbox. Newspaper editors, police departments, and citizens had been expressing these fears to the mayor and the common council of Chicago for years. In response, the local government had replaced the volunteer fire department with professional firefighters but did nothing to take down or forbid wooden structures. Property owners did not

11

Stacks of wood in Chicago's lumber district provided easy fuel for the Great Fire.

want building restrictions. They preferred wood because it was more easily available and generally less expensive than other materials.

Though no longer staffed by volunteers, the fire department was still lacking in other ways. Chicago had 330,000 residents but only 185 professional firefighters.

The firefighters' gear was up-to-date, but there was not enough of it. The water supply was also insufficient. Fire hydrants were too far apart. People shared ideas on how to improve the situation. One suggestion was to place floating fire engines in the river.

This fire engine was used during the time of the Great Fire.

In 1859, a fire that started in a stable burned five blocks of downtown Chicago.

14

Chicago residents had even more reasons to worry. Major fires had previously struck their city in 1839 and 1857, and smaller fires were practically a daily occurrence. Twenty smaller fires broke out in the first week of October 1871 alone. The most damaging of these started in a boiler room of a mill on Chicago's West Side after 10 P.M. on Saturday, October 7.

The fire department battled the boiler room blaze for more than 16 hours. That fire scorched four city blocks and damaged some of the fire department's equipment, including trucks and hoses. By Sunday afternoon, the understaffed fire department was exhausted. They did not know it yet, but they would not get to rest that night. The Great Fire was soon to begin.

THE COW

Laborer Patrick O'Leary and his wife Catherine were immigrants from Ireland. They lived with their five children on Chicago's West Side, less than a mile (1.6 km) from the center of town. Their working-class neighborhood was densely populated, and the streets were narrow. The O'Learys crowded into two rooms at the back of a cottage and rented the front room to another family. Behind the cottage stood a two-story barn—home to five cows, a calf, and a horse. Mrs. O'Leary ran a milk business out of the barn.

A little past 9 P.M. on the night of October 8, all of the O'Learys were sleeping when a man named Daniel Sullivan and another man came to their door. Mr. O'Leary got up and went outside with them. Seconds later, he rushed back shouting, "Kate, the barn is afire!" Terrified, Mrs. O'Leary ran to see for herself.

The fire had already spread from their barn to a

neighbor's barn and a shed. Mrs. O'Leary later described it as burning every which way and making a sound like a cannon. "The roar of the fire, you never heard such a thing," she said. All Mrs. O'Leary's animals except her calf were killed. Though the O'Learys' barn was reduced to ashes, their cottage was unharmed.

The suspected cause of the fire has become a legend. According to a now-famous story, one of Mrs. O'Leary's

The O'Leary home, shown here shortly after the fire, escaped destruction.

cows kicked over a lit lantern that she had accidentally left in the barn, igniting the hay. This explanation has been popular ever since, even though Mrs. O'Leary made no mention of a lantern when she testified to the Board of Police and Fire Commissioners. She further said that she

This painting shows Mrs. O'Leary and her cow at the very moment the fire started.

and her family did not cause the fire and did not even know about it until Sullivan told them. She did not know if anyone else had been in the barn that night. The family renting the front of the cottage did have guests over earlier, and although a neighbor later told Mrs. O'Leary that one of the guests had gone into the barn, that was never proven. The only facts that have been widely accepted are where and when the fire started. Though other theories exist, the true circumstances of the beginning of the Great Chicago Fire may never be known.

Yet once the fire was discovered, its cause did not matter—only controlling it did. The engine company nearest to the O'Leary residence was six blocks away, but it was an engine company 11 blocks away that first noticed the smoke and sent firefighters. A watchman at the court-house also caught sight of smoke, but he thought it was lingering from the boiler room fire the night before. That fire had originated 10 blocks from the O'Leary barn. When he figured out that the smoke came from a new fire,

19

he sent backup—but to the wrong location a mile (1.6 km) away. Firefighters arrived at the O'Learys 10 to 15 minutes after the fire was reported. By then, the blaze had grown much larger. A high wind blew from the southwest, pushing the fire directly toward the center of the city.

Wind helped the fire spread quickly through the "Windy City."

THE NIGHT CHICAGO DIED

The fire spread alarmingly fast. A whirling wind whipped
pieces of burning wood onto neighboring houses. One by
one, the wooden frame houses burst into flame, burning
from top to bottom. By 10:30 P.M., Chicago's West Side was
in shambles. Mills and factories were burned to the
ground. The fire raged out of control, hopping from roof
to roof and racing along wooden sidewalks.

During the early stages of the fire, some people did
not feel threatened. They looked for someplace to watch it.
In most cases, however, the approaching fire brought utter
chaos. From the moment anyone saw, heard, or smelled
the fire, the air was pierced with shrieks, wails, and the
loud crackle of the fire itself.

As reality sank in, people faced the agonizing
decision of what to take and what to leave behind.
Some loaded as much as they could into a wagon only
to abandon it all later because it slowed them down.

Some buried prized possessions hoping to return for them later. Many took nothing.

Some people were trapped in their homes when the fire hit. Others got out in time only to be crushed in the desperate mobs clogging the bridges that led across the Chicago River. People shoved their way out of the city in whatever direction they could. The ground was littered with possessions that people had taken but later discarded,

People carried valuable possessions with them as they tried to escape the fire.

from pets to paintings. The clutter tripped people trying to escape and blocked firefighters from doing their job.

By midnight, the fire had jumped the south branch of the Chicago River. By 1:30 A.M., it swept into the business district. Hotels, offices, and banks were consumed by flames. Inside the burning courthouse, which also housed a jail, the watchman escaped by sliding down the railings. The prisoners screamed to be released. The

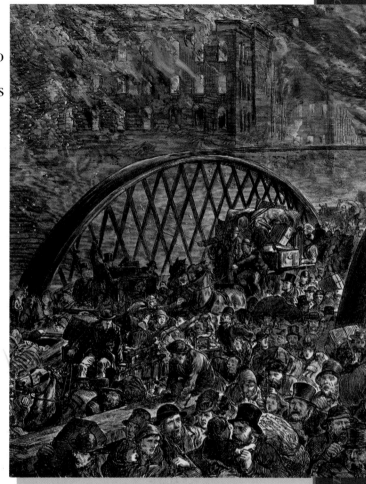

Chicago citizens crossed the Randolph Street Bridge to escape the fire.

most dangerous prisoners were taken out in shackles, but many were allowed to go free. Shortly after 2 A.M., the massive bell atop the courthouse tower crashed through what

23

was left of the building. Then the smoldering tower collapsed with a thunderous sound that people heard a mile (1.6 km) away.

The disaster created both heroes and villains out of ordinary Chicago residents. Among the heroes were fire-fighters, many of whom had families of their own to protect but honored their duty to serve the community. Many average citizens risked their own lives to help others. Some people carried the crippled or injured. There were stories of jewelry store owners who gave away their

Chicago's courthouse (left, before the fire) was reduced to rubble by the fire.

merchandise rather than let it burn. However, others got drunk, looted stores, or hijacked carts of escaping people. Most criminals were not violent, such as those with wagons who offered to drive people's possessions to safety for outrageous prices—and then stole them.

As thousands of people fled north, the inferno chased them, showing little sign of weakening. Even the river caught fire because of the greasy pollution that had collected in it. People on the North

Firemen worked long and hard to battle the Great Chicago Fire.

Side were asleep, unaware of the fire coming their way. It ripped into their community around 3 A.M.

25

The fire jumped the Chicago River and began to burn the North Side.

The western outskirts of Chicago were still prairie. Throughout the wee hours of the night, more and more weary people shuffled to that barren stretch of land. People also flocked to patches of lakeshore within the city. These spots seemed safe since there was little there that could

burn. Before the fire, everyone was either rich or poor.
Now, for the moment, they were all the same. People from
all backgrounds huddled next to one another on the sand,
suffering and afraid, watching much of their city flicker
and sputter into nothingness.

Fire victims gathered in a makeshift camp on Lake Michigan's shore.

FIREPROOF SPIRIT

The fire was still finding more to devour on the North Side past noon on Monday, eventually reaching the northern limit of the city. From warehouse to mansion, all buildings were vulnerable. The North Side was the last part of the city to burn, but it was the hardest hit.

Mercifully, rain began to fall close to midnight on October 9. By Tuesday morning, the flames had been extinguished. In a little over 24 hours, the cityscape of Chicago had changed dramatically. It was now a blackened, steaming wasteland that smelled of burned wood and earth.

More than 300 people died in the fire, and many more were hurt. The fire had wiped out an area approximately 4 miles (6.4 km) long and 1 mile (1.6 km) wide, totaling more than 2,000 acres (800 hectares). At least 90,000 people were homeless. Nearly 18,000 buildings were gone. Property damage was $200 million.

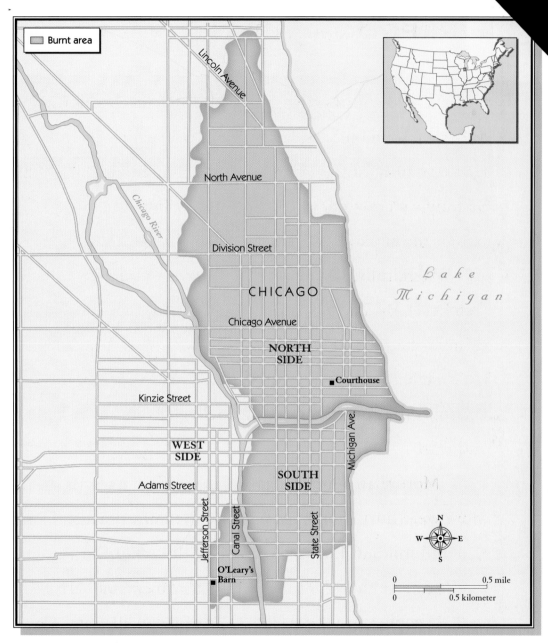

The Great Fire destroyed much of the city of Chicago.

The walls of Chicago's First National Bank survived the fire.

Though the devastation was extensive, parts of the city were not damaged, particularly the industrial sections west and south of the burned region. But wherever the city was damaged by fire, recovery began immediately. The city was not fireproof, but the spirit of its people was.

Rebuilding the city was a colossal task, but

Chicagoans wasted no time. Within a week, they had put up thousands of temporary structures. Other states and countries sent food, clothing, and money. Relief organizations provided aid and vaccinated thousands against small-pox. Two Chicago newspapers were able to put issues out on Monday, and most others resumed publishing on

Relief organizations offered fire victims clothing, food, and other assistance.

31

Wednesday and Thursday. An editorial in the October 11 *Chicago Tribune* read, "Let us all cheer up, save what is yet left, and we shall come out all right."

Amid the good works and inspiring words, some people tried to take advantage of the wounded city. In the days after the fire, rumors of looting and robbing were widespread, although few people actually saw this. Business owners hired Allan Pinkerton, founder of the Pinkerton National Detective Agency, to station his detectives at the remains of stores and banks. The federal government sent troops to help maintain order. Despite the hazards, the city was unified in its determination to dig out from under the rubble.

One incident that demonstrated the optimism of Chicago has become famous among local residents. The day after the fire, a businessman named William Kerfoot converted a shack into a makeshift office. He posted on the door a handwritten sign that read, "All gone but WIFE CHILDREN and ENERGY," and he got back to work.

Businessmen such as William Kerfoot expressed Chicago citizens' determination to return to normal life after the fire.

THE REAL CAUSE

As quickly as the citizens of Chicago began rebuilding their city, they began debating the cause of its destruction. The discussion has continued to the present day. The O'Leary cow theory may be the most familiar, but many researchers do not feel it is the most likely. Many people were at fault for allowing the city to be built in such a careless way. It is often human nature, however, to want to find an individual responsible for a mistake.

Late 19th-century Chicago was not a friendly time and place for many ethnic and religious groups. Prejudice was often aimed at immigrants and Catholics, and the O'Learys were both. They were also part of the lower class. Mrs. O'Leary and her cow may have been blamed for the fire simply because it was convenient. Forty years after the fire, a reporter named Michael Ahern said that he had invented the cow story, and several others made the same claim after him. These claims may or may not be true, but

34

AMERICAN CITIZENS!

We appeal to you in all calmness. Is it not time to pause ? Already the enemies of our dearest institutions, like the foreign spies in the Trojan horse of old, are within our gates. They are disgorging themselves upon us, at the rate of HUNDREDS OF THOUSANDS EVERY YEAR ! They aim at nothing short of conquest and supremacy over us.

A PAPER ENTITLED THE

AMERICAN PATRIOT.

IN FAVOR OF

The protection of American Mechanics against Foreign Pauper Labor.

Foreigners having a residence in the country of 21 years before voting.

Our present Free School System.

Carrying out the laws of the State, as regards sending back Foreign Paupers and Criminals.

OPPOSED TO

Papal Aggression & Roman Catholicism.

Foreigners holding office.

Raising Foreign Military Companies in the United States.

Nunneries and the Jesuits.

To being taxed for the support of Foreign paupers millions of dollars yearly.

To secret Foreign Orders in the U. S.

We are burdened with enormous taxes by foreigners. We are corrupted in the morals of our youth. We are interfered with in our government. We are forced into collisions with other nations. We are tampered with in our religion. We are injured in our labor. We are assailed in our freedom of speech.

☞The PATRIOT is Published by J. E. Farwell & Co., 32 Congress St., Boston, And for Sale at the Periodical Depots in this place. Single copies 4 Cents.

This newspaper expressed the anti-Catholic views that were common at the time.

they certainly add more layers to the mystery.

There are a number of other theories about the cause

of the fire. One is that the fire started with a spark blown from a chimney. Another is that someone dropped a cigarette in the wrong place. Some people suspected that the fire might be a terrorist attack.

A final theory blamed the fire on a fragment from a comet, which plummeted to Earth, landed in the Chicago

Made of ice and dust, comets become fiery when they enter Earth's atmosphere.

area, and set off the blaze. Strangely, two other Midwestern towns also burned to the ground on October 8, 1871. One was Peshtigo, Wisconsin, where approximately 1,500 people died in the fire—many more than in Chicago. The other town to suffer from fire that day was Holland, Michigan, though that was a smaller blaze. Because all three fires started in the same part of the country on the same night, some historians believe it was indeed a splintering comet passing over the area that caused them.

Nevertheless, many historians today suspect that the true cause of the fire was Daniel Sullivan, the man who reported the fire to the O'Learys. They believe Sullivan sneaked into the O'Learys' barn to steal milk from the cows. Before his death, he confessed that he was responsible. That does not mean it is true, but evidence now does seem to point to Sullivan as the culprit. In 1997 the Chicago City Council officially declared Mrs. O'Leary innocent of starting the Great Fire.

A BRAND-NEW CITY

By 1875, few signs remained of the fire's devastation. Rather than duplicate what it once was, Chicago reinvented itself as a modern city built tall and sturdy out of stone and steel. Most people felt the new Chicago was better than it was before the fire. In 1885, Chicago erected

Chicago City Hall was completely rebuilt after the fire.

38

Chicago's State Street was rebuilt with buildings that were larger and grander than before.

the first skyscraper—not only the first in Chicago but the
first in the world. Many more skyscrapers followed. By
1890, the population of Chicago passed 1 million.

In 1893, Chicago hosted the World's Columbian Exposition, a large fair that lasted several months. More than 25 million people attended the fair to enjoy exhibits on science, culture, and other subjects. Chicago proudly showed the people of the world how successfully it had overcome disaster.

The citizens of Chicago would always mourn those

40

Many new buildings were built for the 1893 Columbian Exposition.

A sculpture outside the Chicago Fire Academy commemorates the fire and its victims.

who died, but the reborn city would be an ongoing testa-
ment to their memory. As a song written after the fire pro-
claimed, Chicago was the "Queen of the West once more."

41

GLOSSARY

common council—the lawmaking branch of a local government

engine company—a unit of a fire department

hub—a center of activity

immigrants—people who move from one country to live permanently in another

inferno—a severe fire

laborer—a person who does unskilled physical work

makeshift—something put together to be used in an emergency

tinderbox—a container of material that starts a fire

DID YOU KNOW?

- Though the fire destroyed many businesses, it also created new ones. Some people sold items they found in the rubble of the fire. The great courthouse bell was melted down and turned into souvenirs such as coins and small versions of the bell.

- After the fire, people dumped tons of debris into Lake Michigan, which changed the shape of its shoreline.

- No photographs of the Great Fire are known to exist, although there are both photos and film of the rebuilding.

- In the early 1960s, Chicago built a fire academy on the block where the Great Fire began. The spot where the fire is said to have started is marked on the floor of the academy.

- In 1971, Chicago marked the 100th anniversary of the fire with a fire prevention parade and other events. The big finish was a fireworks display of a cow knocking over a lantern and starting a fire.

- Catherine O'Leary wanted to avoid attention after the fire. Every October, the press tried to interview her, but she always turned them down.

IMPORTANT DATES

Timeline

1839	Fires wreck parts of Chicago, leading some citizens to warn the local government that a larger one could destroy the entire city.
1871	On October 8, a fire breaks out on the West Side of Chicago, most likely in the O'Leary family's barn. It rages through Chicago, destroying much of the city.
1875	After rebuilding, few signs of the fire's damage are visible in Chicago.
1885	The world's first skyscraper goes up in Chicago.
1893	Chicago hosts the World's Columbian Exposition. The world sees that the rebuilt city is flourishing.
1971	Chicago acknowledges the centennial of the Great Fire with a series of events.
1997	Chicago clears the name of Catherine O'Leary, officially stating she did not start the fire.

Important People

Michael Ahern (1850–1927)

Reporter for the Chicago Republican *newspaper at the time of the Great Fire who later said he had invented the story about Mrs. O'Leary's cow starting the blaze*

William Kerfoot (1837–1918)

Businessman who reopened his real estate office in a temporary structure the day after the fire

Patrick O'Leary (1819?–1894) and Catherine O'Leary (1818?–1895)

Irish couple in whose barn the Great Chicago Fire most likely began

Allan Pinkerton (1819–1884)

Founder of the Pinkerton National Detective Agency whose detectives helped monitor crime in Chicago after the Great Fire

Daniel Sullivan (1847–1905)

Neighbor of the O'Learys who alerted them to the fire and later confessed to starting it

WANT TO KNOW MORE?

At the Library

Balcavage, Dynise. *The Great Chicago Fire*. Philadelphia: Chelsea House
    Publications, 2001.

Cromie, Robert. *The Great Chicago Fire*. Nashville, Tenn.: Rutledge Hill
    Press, 1994.

Murphy, Jim. *The Great Fire*. New York: Scholastic, 1995.

On the Web

For more information on the *Great Chicago Fire*, use FactHound

to track down Web sites related to this book.

1. Go to *www.facthound.com*

2. Type in a search word related to this book

    or this book ID: 0756512638

3. Click on the *Fetch It* button.

Your trusty FactHound will fetch the best Web sites for you!

On the Road

Chicago Fire Academy

558 W. DeKoven St.

Chicago, IL 60607

312/747-7239

To see the spot at which the fire is
thought to have started, as well as a
sculpture commemorating the fire

Chicago Fire Museum

St. Gabriel's Roman Catholic Church
and School

4522 S. Wallace

Chicago, IL 60609

773/268-9595

To tour a museum dedicated to the
Great Fire

Look for more We the People books about this era:

Angel Island

*Great Women of the Suffrage
 Movement*

The Harlem Renaissance

The Haymarket Square Tragedy

The Hindenburg

Industrial America

The Johnstown Flood

The Lowell Mill Girls

Roosevelt's Rough Riders

A complete list of We the People titles is available on our Web site:
www.compasspointbooks.com

INDEX

Ahern, Michael, 34
American Civil War, 8

Board of Police and Fire
    Commissioners, 18–19
Bradwell, Bessie, 4–5, 7
Bradwell, James, 4, 6, 7
Bradwell, Myra, 4, 6

Catholicism, 34
Chicago City Council, 37
Chicago River, 10, 22, 23, 25
Chicago Tribune newspaper, 32
comets, 36–37
common council, 11
courthouse, 23–24
criminals, 23, 25

engine companies, 19

factories, 8–9, 30
fire departments, 11, 12, 15, 19
fire engines, 13
fire hydrants, 13
firefighters, 11, 12–13, 19–20, 23,
    24

German immigrants, 8

heroism, 24–25
Holland, Michigan, 37

immigrants, 8, 34
Irish immigrants, 8, 34

Kerfoot, William, 32

Lake Michigan, 10
lakefront, 6, 26
looting, 25, 32

meatpacking plants, 8

newspapers, 11, 31–32
nicknames, 10
North Side, 8, 25, 28

O'Leary, Catherine, 16, 17–19, 34,
    37
O'Leary, Patrick, 16

Peshtigo, Wisconsin, 37
Pinkerton, Allan, 32

Pinkerton National Detective
    Agency, 32
pollution, 25
population, 39
prairie, 26
property damage, 28

railroads, 8
rainfall, 11, 28
reconstruction, 30–31, 38–39
relief organizations, 31
Russian immigrants, 8

skyscrapers, 39
songs, 8, 41
South Side, 8
Sullivan, Daniel, 16, 37

West Side, 8, 16, 21
wood, 11, 12, 21, 28
World's Columbian Exposition, 40

About the Author

Marc Tyler Nobleman is the author of more than 40 books for young people. He writes regularly for *Nickelodeon Magazine* and has written for The History Channel. He is also a cartoonist whose single panels have appeared in more than 100 international publications including *The Wall Street Journal*, *Good Housekeeping*, and *Forbes*. He lives with his wife and daughter in Connecticut.